Evidence-Based Inquiry
Using Primary Sources

Grade 1

Credits
Author: Jeanette Moore Ritch, MS Ed.
Copy Editor: Karen Seberg

Visit *carsondellosa.com* for correlations to Common Core, state, national, and Canadian provincial standards.

Carson-Dellosa Publishing, LLC
PO Box 35665
Greensboro, NC 27425 USA
carsondellosa.com

ISBN 978-1-4838-2396-6
01-106157784

Table of Contents

Introduction

The primary sources shown in this book represent chunks of real life. They are photos of actual people, posters that once hung on storefronts, paintings that interpret history, and ads or articles taken from newspapers in circulation in another era. All primary sources shown here are from the archives of the Library of Congress.

This book includes 15 primary sources. Each primary source selection is accompanied by the same story written at three levels (below grade level, on grade level, and above grade level) for differentiation. Distribute the versions according to students' abilities. The final page of each unit offers prompts and questions about the primary source and/or story and can be used for all levels with some assistance.

This book is full of opportunities for inquiry-based learning. Inquiry-based learning is a process of active learning that greatly improves reading comprehension skills. Allow the primary sources reproduced on these pages to speak for themselves. Then, allow the natural curiosity of students to do the rest. Allow time for discovery.

The role of the teacher in inquiry-based learning is that of facilitator. Teachers are encouraged to first present the primary source without much accompanying information. Encourage students to ask questions, look for answers, and form relationships between the past and the present. Prompt students to think critically about what they see. Let them make inferences from the details, share varying points of view, draw conclusions, and connect known facts with details in the visuals shown.

Performance Rubric

Use this rubric as a guide for assessing students' engagement with each primary source unit.

4	_____ Notes details and evaluates primary source critically
	_____ Displays avid curiosity about photo and topic
	_____ Makes or disproves connections between primary source and personal experiences or prior knowledge
	_____ Exhibits high-level thinking skills when responding to *Investigate, Question,* and *Understand* prompts
3	_____ Notes details and evaluates primary source superficially
	_____ Displays average curiosity about photo and topic
	_____ Makes mostly obvious connections between primary source and personal experiences or prior knowledge
	_____ Responds with adequate insight to *Investigate, Question,* and *Understand* prompts
2	_____ Notes some details but does not evaluate primary source
	_____ Displays some curiosity about photo and topic
	_____ Makes few connections between primary source and personal experiences or prior knowledge
	_____ Responds without insight or high-level thinking to *Investigate, Question,* and *Understand* prompts
1	_____ Notes few details and does not evaluate primary source
	_____ Displays no curiosity about photo and topic
	_____ Makes no connections between primary source and personal experiences or prior knowledge
	_____ Shows little interest in or is unable to respond thoughtfully to *Investigate, Question,* and *Understand* prompts

How to Use This Book

Teachers may wish to prompt students to study each primary source before reading the accompanying text. Students can write or ask questions as they study the documents or photographs. Spark their curiosity with discussion about the elements of the primary source. Students may then discover more information in the text. An inquiry page follows each set of texts and provides three levels of prompts: *Investigate, Question,* and *Understand.* Allow time and opportunity for students to answer their own questions and to find out more in books, magazines, and on safe Internet sources.

Fire Trucks Long Ago

The steam fire engine was on a fire truck. It was big. The engine got hot. Steam came out of the pipe. The engine pumped water to put out fires. Firemen put out fires in homes. They put out fires in buildings. The steam engine was helpful.

This steam engine is from 1900. It is in New York City. It has wheels. It has a fire hose. It is pulled by horses. The horses are fast! They help get the firemen to the fire. The people watch them go!

Library of Congress, LC-USZ62-26744

Fire Trucks Long Ago

The steam fire engine was big. It was on a fire truck. The engine got hot. When it was hot, it made steam. The steam engine pumped water. The water went through hoses. Firemen used the water to put out fires.

Steam fire engines were used in cities. Firemen drove the engines. They put out fires in homes. They put out fires in buildings. The steam engine was helpful.

This steam fire engine is from 1900. It is in New York City. The steam engine has wheels. It is pulled by horses. The three horses are fast! They help get the firemen to the fire. The people watch the firemen and the steam engine go!

Library of Congress, LC-USZ62-26744

Fire Trucks Long Ago

Steam fire engines were used on fire trucks. They pumped water for firemen. The water went through big hoses. The water put out fires. The steam engine was pulled by horses. It was not as fast as a fire truck is today.

Steam fire engines were important in cities. The engines were stored in firehouses. Firemen drove the engines. They put out fires for people. They put out fires in homes. They put out fires in buildings. The steam engine was helpful to firemen.

This photo is from 1900. That is over 100 years ago! There are three white horses. They are pulling the engine. They are going fast down the street. People watch it go, go, go!

Library of Congress, LC-USZ62-26744

Name _____

Fire Trucks Long Ago

 Investigate

1. What do you see in this photo?

   _____

   _____

2. What did you see first? Why?

   _____

   _____

 Question

3. Look at the photo. What do you want to learn more about?

   _____

   _____

4. Have you ever seen a fire truck? When?

   _____

   _____

 Understand

5. Why do you think there are three horses?

   _____

   _____

6. Why is it called a **steam** fire engine?

   _____

   _____

Milk Trucks

Milk trucks had a big job. They delivered milk to people. The milk was from a dairy farm. The dairy farm had cows. The cows made milk. The farmer took the milk. He put the milk into bottles. The bottles were made of glass.

The milk went into a milk truck. A man drove the milk to towns. The milk was fresh. People liked drinking the milk in their homes.

This photo is from 1910. The truck has four tires. It is black. It is shaped like a rectangle. The driver is a man. He is wearing a hat. He has a uniform. He is holding the milk. Yum!

© Carson-Dellosa • CD-104859 • Evidence-Based Inquiry Using Primary Sources

Milk Trucks

Milk trucks had a big job. They delivered milk to people. The milk was from a dairy farm. The dairy farm had cows. The cows made milk. The farmer took the milk. He put the milk into bottles. The bottles were made of glass.

The milk bottles went into a milk truck. The driver drove the milk to towns. The milk was fresh. People enjoyed drinking the milk delivered to their homes.

This photo is from 1910. The truck has four thin tires. It is black. It is shaped like a rectangle. The driver is wearing a hat. He has a uniform. He is holding bottles of milk. Yum!

Milk Trucks

Milk trucks delivered a tasty treat. About 100 years ago, they delivered milk. The milk was from a dairy farm. The dairy farm had cows. The cows would make milk. The farmer took the milk and put it into bottles. The bottles were made out of glass.

The milk bottles went into a milk truck. The driver took the milk to neighborhoods in towns. The milk was fresh. People enjoyed drinking the milk delivered to their homes.

This photo is from 1910. The truck has four thin tires. It is black. It is shaped like a rectangle. The driver is wearing a hat. He is wearing a uniform. He is holding bottles of milk. Yum!

Library of Congress, LC-DIG-npcc-32125

Milk Trucks

 Investigate

1. What do you see in this photo?

   _____

   _____

2. What did you see first? Why?

   _____

   _____

 Question

3. Look at the picture. What do you want to learn more about?

   _____

   _____

4. Have you ever seen a milk truck? When?

   _____

   _____

Understand

5. Why do you think the milk was put into glass bottles?

   _____

   _____

6. How is this truck different from a truck you have seen?

   _____

   _____

Wright's Flights

There were two brothers. They lived in Ohio. The boys were Orville and Wilbur Wright. They loved to read and play. They read about kites and birds. They loved things that fly. One day, their dad gave them a flying toy. It was made out of cork, paper, and a rubber band. They wanted to fly one day too.

The boys went to school. When they grew up, they owned a bicycle shop. They had the idea to make a plane. First, they made gliders. These were like kites that people could hang onto. Then, the Wright brothers made a plane. It crashed. They tried again. They did it! They made the first plane.

This photo is from 1909. The man is watching the plane. It is over New York Harbor. It has wings. It has an engine. But, the plane looks different from airplanes today. There goes the plane! Up, up, and away!

Library of Congress, LC-USZ62-5887

Wright's Flights

There were two brothers. They lived in Ohio. Their names were Orville and Wilbur Wright. They read about kites and birds because they loved things that fly. One day, their dad gave them a flying toy. It was made out of bamboo, cork, paper, and a rubber band. They loved the idea of flying. They wanted to fly one day too.

The boys went to school. When they grew up, they owned a bicycle shop. They thought of creating an airplane. First, they made gliders. Then, the Wright brothers made a real flying plane. It crashed, but they tried again. They were successful. They made the first plane! Their invention would change the world.

This photo is from 1909. The man is watching the plane. It is over New York Harbor. It has wings. It has an engine. But, the plane looks different from airplanes today. There goes the plane! Up, up, and away!

Library of Congress, LC-USZ62-5887

Wright's Flights

There were two brothers in Ohio. Their names were Orville and Wilbur Wright. They read about kites and birds because they loved things that fly. One day, their dad gave them a flying toy. It was made out of bamboo, cork, paper, and a rubber band. They loved the idea of flying. They wanted to fly one day themselves. But, no person had ever flown.

The boys went to school. They were excellent students. When they grew up, they owned a bicycle shop. They thought of creating an airplane. First, they made gliders. Then, the Wright brothers made a real flying plane. It crashed, but they tried again. They were successful. They had made the first plane. Their invention would change the world!

This photo is from 1909. The man is watching the plane. It is over New York Harbor. It has wings and an engine. But, the plane looks different from airplanes today.

Library of Congress, LC-USZ62-5887

Name _____

Wright's Flights

 Investigate

1. What do you see in this photo?

_____

_____

2. What did you see first? Why?

_____

_____

 Question

3. Look at the photo. What do you want to learn more about?

_____

_____

4. Have you ever seen an airplane? When?

_____

_____

Understand

5. How do you know the brothers liked flying?

_____

_____

6. How is this plane different from planes today?

_____

_____

Smell and Touch the World

When Helen Keller was born, she could see. She could hear. When she was a toddler, she got sick. Then, she could not hear. She could not see. Her mom and dad wanted to help her. They sent her to a new school. It was far away.

Helen's teacher was named Anne. She showed Helen how to read. Helen read with her hands and fingers. She read dots, or bumps, that were on paper. The print is called Braille. Helen learned outside too. She liked nature. Helen liked flowers and trees.

This photo is from 1904. Helen Keller has a book on her lap. She is reading with her hands. She is smelling a rose. She is using her nose and hands to learn. Do you do this too?

Helen Keller, No. 8

Library of Congress, LC-DIG-ppmsca-23661

Smell and Touch the World

Helen Keller was from Alabama. Helen was sick when she was small. She was not able to hear anymore. She was not able to see anymore. Her parents wanted to help her. They sent her to a school. Helen's life changed.

Anne Sullivan was Helen's teacher. She taught Helen to read. Anne showed Helen how to read with her hands and fingers. She read dots, or bumps, that were on paper. The print is called Braille. Helen learned from nature too. Helen liked flowers and trees.

This photo is from 1904. Helen has a book. She is reading with her hands. She is wearing a white shirt. She is smelling a rose. She is using her nose and hands to learn about the world. Do you do this too?

Helen Keller, No. 8

Library of Congress, LC-DIG-ppmsca-23661

Smell and Touch the World

Helen Keller was from Alabama. Helen was sick when she was a little girl. She was not able to hear or see anymore. Her parents sent her to a special school. Helen's life changed forever.

Anne Sullivan was Helen's teacher. She taught Helen how to read. Anne showed Helen how to read with her hands and fingers. Helen read dots, or bumps, that were on paper. This writing is called Braille. Anne also helped Helen learn from nature. Helen liked flowers and trees.

This photo is from 1904. Helen Keller has a book on her lap. She is reading with her hands. She is wearing a pretty white shirt. She is smelling a rose. The roses are in a glass vase. She is using her senses to understand the world. Do you do this too?

Helen Keller, No. 8

Library of Congress, LC-DIG-ppmsca-23661

Name _____

Smell and Touch the World

🔍 Investigate

1. What do you see in this photo?

_____

_____

2. What did you see first? Why?

_____

_____

❓ Question

3. Look at the photo. What do you want to learn more about?

_____

_____

4. Does the photo show that Helen is blind? Explain your answer.

_____

_____

💡 Understand

5. Look at the book. How is it different from your books?

_____

_____

6. How do you use your nose to learn?

_____

_____

Ben Franklin

Ben Franklin was a great man. He was an American. He liked to read. He was a writer. He wrote news. He wrote books. He started a hospital. He started a school.

Ben had many jobs! He was an inventor too. Ben worked with electricity! He made a stove. He made glasses. He wanted to help people have good lives. He made good things.

This picture is from 1847. It is a picture of Ben. Ben is in a chair. He has books. He has a feather pen. There is a globe on the floor. Look behind Ben. Do you see a window? Look at the storm in the sky! The artist shows many things that Ben used.

Library of Congress, LC-USZ62-19451

Ben Franklin

Ben Franklin was a great man. He was an American. He was a writer. He wrote a newspaper. He wrote books. He started a hospital. He started a school.

Ben had many jobs! He also made things no one had made before. This means he was an inventor. Ben worked with electricity. He made a stove. He made eyeglasses. He wanted to help people have good lives. He made useful things.

This picture is from 1847. It is a picture of Ben. Ben is sitting in a chair. He has a compass. There is a globe by his feet. Look behind Ben. Do you see the window? There is a storm in the sky! The artist drew many things that Ben worked with.

Library of Congress, LC-USZ62-19451

Ben Franklin

Ben Franklin was a great American. He was a writer. He wrote a newspaper. He started a hospital. He even started a school!

Ben had many jobs. He also made things no one had made before. He was an inventor. Ben worked with electricity. He made a stove. He made special eyeglasses too. He wanted people to have better lives. He made useful things.

This picture is from 1847. It is a portrait of Ben. Ben is sitting in a chair. He is holding a compass. There is a globe by his feet. Look behind Ben. Do you see the window? There is a storm in the sky! The artist drew many things that Ben worked with.

Library of Congress, LC-USZ62-19451

Ben Franklin

 Investigate

1. What do you see in this picture?

   _____

   _____

2. What did you see first? Why?

   _____

   _____

? Question

3. Look at the picture. What do you want to learn more about?

   _____

   _____

4. Who was Ben Franklin?

   _____

   _____

Understand

5. This picture was made more than 50 years after Ben died. What did the artist think was important to tell about Ben?

   _____

   _____

6. What would you ask Ben if you met him?

   _____

   _____

Plants and Peanuts

George Washington Carver was from Missouri. He had a brother. His name was James. Mary was their mom. She died. So, Susan and Moses Carver were their new mom and dad. George was smart. He liked to read. He liked animals. He liked plants a lot.

George went to school. He looked at plants. He learned about plants. He finished school. Then, he was a teacher. George spoke about plants. He had class outside. George liked the peanut plant best. He made things from peanuts. He made oil. He made dye. He made peanut butter!

This photo is from 1906. It is a picture of George. He is in a field. He has a hat. Look at his hand. He is holding a piece of dirt. He knew how to grow plants!

Library of Congress, LC-USZ62-114302

Plants and Peanuts

George Washington Carver was born in Missouri. His brother was James. Mary was their mom. She died. So, Moses and Susan Carver became their new parents. George was smart. He liked to read. He liked animals and plants.

George went to school. He learned about many plants. He did a good job. Then, he became a teacher. He helped students. George spoke about plants. He had class outside. George liked the peanut plant best. He made many things from peanuts. He made oil. He made dye. He made peanut butter!

This photo is from 1906. It is a picture of George. He is in a field. He has a hat. He is holding some dirt. He knew how to grow many plants!

Library of Congress, LC-USZ62-114302

Plants and Peanuts

George Washington Carver was born in Missouri. He is a famous African-American man. He and his brother James lived with Moses and Susan Carver. Their mom, Mary, died. Then, Moses and Susan became their new parents. George loved to read. He liked animals and plants.

When George was older, he went to college. He liked to study plants. He was a teacher. George taught about plants and how they grow. He worked in a lab. George was interested in the peanut plant. Many things could be made from peanuts. He made peanut oil. He made peanut dye. He also made peanut butter!

This photo is from 1906. It is a picture of George. He is standing in a field. He is wearing a suit. He has a hat. He is holding a big clump of soil. He knew how to grow many plants!

Library of Congress, LC-USZ62-114302

Name _____

Plants and Peanuts

 Investigate

1. What do you see in this photo?

   _____

   _____

2. What did you see first? Why?

   _____

   _____

 Question

3. Look at the photo. What do you want to learn more about?

   _____

   _____

4. What plant did George like best? How do you know?

   _____

   _____

 Understand

5. Why is George holding a clump of dirt?

   _____

   _____

6. What would you ask George if you met him?

   _____

   _____

Dodgeball

Girls and boys play sports. Girls and boys played sports years ago. Girls played sports together. They played softball. They played tennis. They played dodgeball.

Dodgeball is a game. There are two teams. One team makes a big circle. One team stands inside of the circle. Players throw the ball. They try to hit someone in the circle. A girl goes to the outside circle when hit. The game goes until one girl is left.

This photo is from 1910. It shows girls. The teacher is there too. They are on a playground. They are playing a game. They are playing dodgeball. They are in a circle. There is a girl in the middle. She has the ball. The girls wear dresses. They are friends. Teams are fun!

Library of Congress, LC-USZ62-70864

Dodgeball

Girls and boys play sports. Girls and boys played sports more than 100 years ago. Girls played sports together. They played softball. They played tennis. They played dodgeball.

Dodgeball is a game. It started long ago. There are two teams. One team makes a big circle. The other team stands inside the circle. Players on the outside throw the ball. They throw the ball at someone inside the circle. If a person in the circle is hit, she goes to the outside team. The game keeps going until one person is left.

This photo is from 1910. It is a picture of a group of girls. The teacher is there too. They are on a playground. They are playing dodgeball. They stand in a circle. The girl in the middle has the ball. The girls are wearing dresses. They are holding hands. They are friends. It is good to play with the team.

Library of Congress, LC-USZ62-70864

Dodgeball

Girls and boys play sports. Girls and boys played sports more than 100 years ago. Girls played sports together. They played softball and tennis. They played basketball. They even played dodgeball.

Dodgeball is a game. It started long ago. There are two teams. One team makes a big circle. The other team stands inside the circle. Players on the outside throw the ball. They throw the ball at someone inside the circle. If a person in the circle is hit, she goes to the outside team. The game keeps going until only one person is left.

This photo is from 1910. It is a picture of a group of girls on a playground. The teacher is there too. They are playing dodgeball. They are standing in a circle. The girl in the middle has the ball. The girls are wearing dresses. They are friends. It is good to cooperate with team members. It is fun to play together.

Library of Congress, LC-USZ62-70864

Name _____

Dodgeball

 Investigate

1. What do you see in this photo?

   _____

   _____

2. What did you see first? Why?

   _____

   _____

 Question

3. Look at the photo. What do you want to learn more about?

   _____

   _____

4. What sports did kids play long ago?

   _____

   _____

 Understand

5. What are the girls wearing?

   _____

   _____

6. Does this look like your playground? Explain your answer.

   _____

   _____

Build an Igloo

Igloo means house. It is an Inuit word. Many Inuit live in Alaska. Alaska is in the North. It is cold. There is lots of snow!

Long ago, the Inuit had three kinds of houses. There was the earth house. It was in the ground. But, the Inuit moved. They moved in the summer. Then, they would use a tent. They moved in the winter. Then, they would build an igloo. The igloo was made of snow. It was shaped like a dome. A dome is a half of a circle. Igloos kept people warm.

This photo is from 1924. People are making an igloo. They have snow. The snow is in blocks. They are rectangles. There are children. There are dogs. Are they sled dogs? It is cold!

Library of Congress, LC-USZ62-135985

Build an Igloo

The word *igloo* means house. It is an Inuit word. Many Inuit live in Alaska. Alaska is in the North. It has cold weather. It has lots of snow!

Long ago, the Inuit had three kinds of houses. There was the earth house. It was partly in the ground. But, the Inuit traveled to hunt. In the summer, they would use a tent. In the winter, they would build an igloo. The igloo was made of snow. It was shaped like a dome. A dome is a half of a circle. Igloos kept people warm. They could build an igloo anywhere.

This photo is from 1924. People are making an igloo. They have blocks of snow. The blocks are rectangles. There are children. There are dogs. Are they sled dogs? It is cold!

Library of Congress, LC-USZ62-135985

Build an Igloo

The word *igloo* means house. It is an Inuit word. Inuit people live in Alaska. Alaska is in the northern part of the world. It has very cold weather. There is lots of snow.

Many years ago, the Inuit had three kinds of houses. There was the earth house. It was partly in the ground. It was made with soil and building materials. But often, Inuit traveled to hunt. They used tents in the summer. In the winter, they built igloos. An igloo is made of snow. It is shaped like a dome. A dome is a half of a sphere. Igloos kept people warm. An igloo could be built anywhere there was enough snow.

This photo is from 1924. People are making an igloo. They have blocks of snow. The blocks are big rectangles. There are children. The children are watching and helping. The people have dogs. Are they sled dogs? It is cold!

Library of Congress, LC-USZ62-135985

Name _____

Build an Igloo

 Investigate

1. What do you see in this photo?

   _____

   _____

2. What did you see first? Why?

   _____

   _____

 **Question**

3. Look at the photo. What do you want to learn more about?

   _____

   _____

4. What is an igloo?

   _____

   _____

 Understand

5. Why was an igloo a good house for an Inuit family?

   _____

   _____

6. Why are the Inuit wearing big coats?

   _____

   _____

Class Time

Most kids learned at home long ago. Home school was popular. Some kids had tutors. Teachers went to homes. Some kids were taught by parents. In the 1800s, kids went to public school. But, not all kids went to school. Some kids worked on farms. Some kids worked in factories.

In 1918, many kids went to school. They learned how to read. They learned how to write. They did math. Most teachers were women.

This photo is from 1899. Girls are in the class. Boys are in the class. Everyone is dressed well! A chalkboard is on the wall. The kids sit at desks. The teacher is a woman. She has a dog. Do you have a dog in your class?

Library of Congress, LC-USZ62-39163

Class Time

Most kids learned at home hundreds of years ago. Home school was very popular. Some kids had tutors. Some kids had teachers come to their homes. Some kids were taught by parents. In the 1800s, kids began to go to public school. But, not all kids went to school. Some kids worked on farms. Some kids worked in factories.

In 1918, many kids had to go to elementary school. They learned to read. They learned to write. They learned math. Most teachers were women.

This photo is from 1899. Girls and boys are in the class. Everyone is dressed up! A chalkboard is on the wall. The kids sit at desks. The teacher is a woman. She has a dog. Do you have a dog in your class?

Library of Congress, LC-USZ62-39163

Class Time

Many kids learned at home hundreds of years ago. Home school was very popular. Some kids had tutors. Some kids had teachers come to their homes. Some kids were taught by their parents. They learned many subjects. In the 1800s, some public schools started. But, not everyone went to school. Some kids worked on farms. Some kids worked in factories.

By 1918, many kids had to go to elementary school. They learned to read. They learned to write. They learned math. They also talked about current events in class. They discussed history too. Most teachers were women.

This photo is from 1899. Girls and boys are in the class. Everyone is dressed up! All of the children are facing forward. A chalkboard is on the wall. The teacher is a woman. She is next to a dog. Do you have a dog in your class?

Library of Congress, LC-USZ62-39163

Class Time

 Investigate

1. What do you see in this photo?

    _____

    _____

2. What did you see first? Why?

    _____

    _____

 Question

3. Look at the photo. What do you want to learn more about?

    _____

    _____

4. What special item is in the classroom? Describe it. Think of a name for it!

    _____

    _____

Understand

5. What are the kids learning about?

    _____

    _____

6. How is your classroom like this classroom? How is it different?

    _____

    _____

Chief American Horse

Chief American Horse lived long ago. He was a leader. He was in a tribe. It was the Sioux tribe. American Horse was an American Indian.

He fought when he was young. He fought the Crow tribe. American Horse was a brave. He was a hunter. He had a bow. He had a quiver. It was a holder. Arrows were in it. The chief liked good schools. His kids went to school. The school was far away. His kids lived there.

This photo is from 1899. The chief wears a headdress. It is a special hat. It has feathers. It has beads. He wears moccasins. The chief wears many special clothes.

Library of Congress, LC-DIG-ppmsca-15856

Chief American Horse

Chief American Horse lived over 100 years ago. He belonged to a tribe. The tribe was called Sioux. He was an American Indian. He was a leader.

He fought when he was young. He fought the Crow tribe. He was a warrior. He was also a hunter. He had a bow. He had a quiver. It was a holder. He had arrows in it. American Horse believed in good schools. His kids went to school. The school was far away. They lived at the school.

This photo is from 1899. The chief wears a headdress. It is a special kind of hat. It has many feathers. It has beads. He has moccasins on his feet. The chief has many special clothes.

Library of Congress, LC-DIG-ppmsca-15856

Chief American Horse

Chief American Horse lived in the 1800s. He was part of a tribe. The tribe was called the Sioux. He was an American Indian. He was a leader.

As a boy, American Horse fought the Crow tribe. He was known to be a great warrior. He was also a hunter. He had a bow. He had arrows. He used a quiver to hold the arrows. The chief believed in good schools. His children went to school. They went to school far away. They lived at their school.

This photo is from 1899. The chief is wearing a headdress. It is a special kind of hat. It has many feathers. He has moccasins on his feet. The chief is wearing many special clothes.

Library of Congress, LC-DIG-ppmsca-15856

Name _____

Chief American Horse

 Investigate

1. What do you see in this photo?

_____

_____

2. What did you see first? Why?

_____

_____

 **Question**

3. Look at the photo. What do you want to learn more about?

_____

_____

4. Have you ever seen a headdress? Where did you see it?

_____

_____

 Understand

5. How can you tell American Horse is a chief?

_____

_____

6. What are moccasins? Do you have any?

_____

_____

Chief Charlot and Family

Chief Charlot led a tribe. The tribe was the Salish tribe. He led the tribe for a long time. He led for 40 years! He lived in Montana.

His people lived in tepees. A tepee is a house. It is an American Indian house. It was made from animal skins. Big sticks held it up. It kept the people warm. It kept them dry. They moved when they hunted. The tepees were moved too.

This photo is from 1908. The chief is with his family. Look behind them. There are mountains. The family wears beads. They have braids. They have feathers. They wear pretty clothes.

Library of Congress, LC-USZ62-55953

Chief Charlot and Family

Chief Charlot was a leader. He led a tribe. The tribe was the Salish tribe. His tribe was also called the Flatheads. He led the tribe for a long time. He led them for 40 years! He lived in Montana.

His people lived in tepees. A tepee is a kind of house. It is an American Indian house. It was made out of animal skins. A tepee's door faced the sun. The tepee helped in bad weather. It kept the people warm. It was easy to move when they hunted.

This photo is from 1908. The chief is with his family. There are mountains behind them. They wear beads. Their hair is in braids. They wear Salish clothes. Look at the designs!

Library of Congress, LC-USZ62-55953

Chief Charlot and Family

Chief Charlot was a leader. He led a tribe. The tribe was the Salish tribe. His tribe was also called the Flatheads. He led the tribe for 40 years! He lived in Montana.

His people lived in tepees. A tepee is one kind of American Indian house. The tepee's door faced the sun. The tepee was made out of animal skins. It protected the Salish from weather. It was easy to move when the Salish hunted.

This photo is from 1908. There are mountains in the background. The chief is with his family. They wear beads. Their hair is in braids. They wear Salish clothes. Look at the designs!

Library of Congress, LC-USZ62-55953

Chief Charlot and Family

 Investigate

1. What do you see in this photo?

_____

_____

2. What did you see first? Why?

_____

_____

 Question

3. Look at the photo. What do you want to learn more about?

_____

_____

4. What is a tepee?

_____

_____

Understand

5. Look at all of the tepees. How is this like your town? How is it different?

_____

_____

6. What are the people wearing? What are they holding?

_____

_____

Cradleboard

The Apache are a tribe. They are American Indians. They live in the Southwest. They live in many places. Some live in the desert. Some live in the plains. Some live in the mountains.

It was special when an Apache baby was born. Its ears were pierced. There was a party. The baby was blessed. The baby was given a cradleboard. It had toys on it. It held the baby. The cradleboard kept the baby safe. It blocked the sun. It protected skin.

This photo is from 1903. The baby is happy. The cradleboard holds the baby. It is made of wood. It is made of cloth. It has leather. There is a blanket. The baby is snug. The girl looks at the baby. The baby makes her smile.

Library of Congress, LC-USZC4-8845

Cradleboard

The Apache people are a tribe. They are American Indians. They live in the Southwest. They live in many places. Some live in the desert. Some live in the plains. Some live in the mountains.

It was special when a baby was born. The Apaches pierced its ears. There was a party. The baby was blessed. The baby was given a cradleboard. It was a wooden holder. It had toys on it. It held the baby. A cradleboard kept the baby safe. It blocked the sun. It protected the baby's skin.

This photo is from 1903. The baby is happy. The baby is in the cradleboard. It is made of wood. It is made of cloth and leather. There is a blanket. The baby is snug. The girl is looking at the baby. She smiles at the baby. Maybe she sings too!

Library of Congress, LC-USZC4-8845

Cradleboard

The Apache people are American Indians. They live in the Southwest. Some live in the desert. Some live in the plains. Some live in the mountains.

Some special things happened when a baby was born in the Apache tribe. They pierced the baby's ears. They gave the baby a blessing. They gave the baby a cradleboard party. Boy babies and girl babies got cradleboards. A cradleboard was a wooden holder. It held the baby tightly. It had toys on it. The cradleboard kept the baby safe. It blocked the sun. It protected the baby's skin.

This photo is from 1903. The baby is happy. The baby is in the cradleboard. It is made out of wood, leather, and cloth. The baby is snug. The girl is looking at the baby. Maybe she sings to the baby too.

Library of Congress, LC-USZC4-8845

Name _____

Cradleboard

 Investigate

1. What do you see in this photo?

_____

_____

2. What did you see first? Why?

_____

_____

 Question

3. Look at the photo. What do you want to learn more about?

_____

_____

4. How do you think a cradleboard is made?

_____

_____

 Understand

5. What did the Apache do for a new baby?

_____

_____

6. How is the baby kept safe in the cradleboard?

_____

_____

Happy New Year!

Do you know about Rosh Hashanah? It is a special holiday. It is the New Year. It is for Jewish people. It can be in September. It can be in October. This holiday is not the same as the New Year in January. But, both are for planning for the year ahead.

Jewish people do not work on this day. They eat bread. They eat apples. They dip them in honey. They go to temple. They pray. They blow a horn. It is from a ram. It is called a *shofar*.

This photo is from 1911. The boy is Jewish. He is wearing a prayer shawl. It is like a blanket. He wears it around his neck. He has a book. The book has prayers. He has a hat. He is dressed well. He celebrates the New Year.

Library of Congress, LC-USZ62-38119

Happy New Year!

Do you know about Rosh Hashanah? It is a holiday. It is the New Year for the Jewish people. It is in September or October. This holiday is not the same as the New Year in January. But, both are for planning for the year ahead.

Jewish people do not work on this day. They eat bread. They eat apples. They dip them in honey. They go to temple. They pray. They blow a ram's horn. It is called a *shofar.*

This photo is from 1911. The boy is Jewish. He is wearing a prayer shawl. It is like a blanket. He wears it around his neck. He has a special book of prayers. He has a hat. He celebrates the New Year.

Library of Congress, LC-USZ62-38119

Happy New Year!

Jewish people have a holiday called Rosh Hashanah. It is the New Year. It can be in September. Sometimes, it is in October. This holiday is not the same as the New Year on the first day of January. But, both are for planning for the year ahead.

Jewish people do not work on this day. They eat bread. They eat apples. They dip them in honey. They go to temple. They pray. They blow a ram's horn. It is called a *shofar*.

This photo is from 1911. The boy is Jewish. He practices Judaism, the Jewish religion. He is wearing a prayer shawl. It is like a blanket. He is wearing it around his neck. He is holding a special book of prayers. He is ready to celebrate the New Year.

Library of Congress, LC-USZ62-38119

Happy New Year!

 Investigate

1. What do you see in this photo?

   _____

   _____

2. What did you see first? Why?

   _____

   _____

 Question

3. Look at the photo. What do you want to learn more about?

   _____

   _____

4. What is the setting for this photo?

   _____

   _____

 Understand

5. Why is the boy wearing a shawl?

   _____

   _____

6. What does he do on Rosh Hashanah?

   _____

   _____

Let's Play

There are five boys. They are playing a game. One boy is on the bottom. He is strong. The other four boys are on the top. They make a shape together. They look like a dragon's head. They might be celebrating Lunar New Year.

The dragon is a special animal. It is special to the Chinese people. It is strong. It is gentle. It is in Chinese art. It is in temples. It is said to be good luck.

This photo is from 1929. The boys are Chinese. They are having fun. The other kids are looking. They are sitting on a wall. The wall is made of rocks. It is fun to watch! Soon it will be their turn to play.

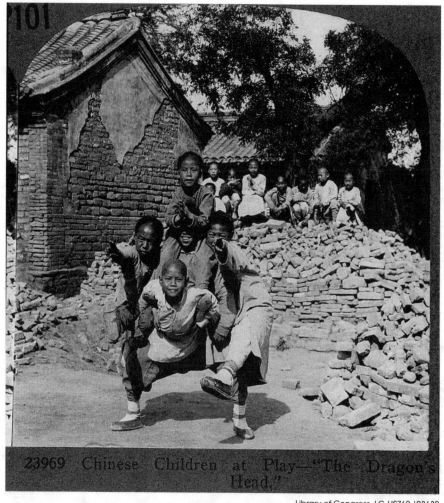

23969 Chinese Children at Play—"The Dragon's Head."

Let's Play

There are five boys. They are playing a game. They work together. One strong boy is on the bottom. The other four boys are on the top. They look like a dragon's head. They might be celebrating Lunar New Year.

The dragon is an important animal for the Chinese people. It is powerful. It is gentle. It is in Chinese art. It is in temples. It is a sign of good luck.

This photo is from 1929. The boys are Chinese. They are playing together. They are having fun. The other kids are looking. They are sitting on a wall. The wall is made of rocks. This looks like it is fun to watch! Maybe they will take the next turn.

23969 Chinese Children at Play—"The Dragon's Head."

Library of Congress, LC-USZ62-103632

Let's Play

There are five boys. The boys are playing a game. They work together. One strong boy is on the bottom. The other four boys are on the top. They are forming part of an animal. They are making a dragon's head. They might be celebrating Lunar New Year.

The dragon is an important animal for the Chinese people. It is powerful, but it is gentle. It is in Chinese paintings. It is made into sculptures. It is in temples. It is a symbol, or sign, of good luck.

This photo is from 1929. The boys are Chinese. They are playing happily together. The other kids are looking as they sit on a wall. The wall is made of rocks. This game looks like it is fun to watch. Maybe the boys watching will take the next turn!

23969 Chinese Children at Play—"The Dragon's Head."

Let's Play

 Investigate

1. What do you see in this photo?

   _____

   _____

2. What did you see first? Why?

   _____

   _____

 Question

3. Look at the photo. What do you want to learn more about?

   _____

   _____

4. What shape are the five boys making? Why?

   _____

   _____

 Understand

5. How do the kids have fun?

   _____

   _____

6. Why are dragons special?

   _____

   _____

Hopi Girls at Home

Look at the two girls. They are at home. They are American Indians. They are part of the Hopi tribe. The girls live in a pueblo. A pueblo is a home. It is made from bricks. The bricks are made from mud and straw. They are dried in the sun.

The Hopis live in Arizona. They live on mesas. A mesa is land that is higher than the land around it. The mesa is near the desert. The land is dry. The air is hot. The sun shines.

This photo is from 1900. The girls are outside. Their hair is black. Their hair is in buns. The buns mean they are not married. The buns are called squash blossoms. They are near a blanket or rug. It has a design. Did they make it?

Library of Congress, LC-USZ62-48382

Hopi Girls at Home

There are two girls. They are at home. They are from the Hopi tribe. The Hopi tribe is American Indian. These girls live in a pueblo building. A pueblo is a home made from adobe bricks. The bricks are made from mud and straw. They are dried in the sun.

The Hopi live on mesas in Arizona. The mesas are raised land. They are above the desert. The land is dry. The air is hot.

This photo is from 1900. The two girls are outside of the pueblo. Their hair is black. Their hair is in buns. The buns mean they are not married. The buns are called squash blossoms. They are near a blanket or rug. It has an interesting design on it. Did they make it?

Hopi Girls at Home

There are two young girls. They are at their home. They are part of the Hopi tribe. The Hopi tribe is American Indian. These girls live in a pueblo building. A pueblo is a home made from adobe bricks, wood, and rocks. Adobe bricks are made from mud and straw. Then, they are dried in the sun.

The Hopi live in Arizona on mesas. The mesas are raised sections of land. They are above the desert. The land is dry and the air is hot.

This photo is from 1900. The two girls are outside of the pueblo. They are on a porch area. Their hair is black. They wear their hair in buns. The buns mean they are not married. The buns are called squash blossoms. The girls are near a blanket or rug. The blanket or rug is hanging over a wall. It has an interesting design on it. Did they make it?

Library of Congress, LC-USZ62-48382

Hopi Girls at Home

 Investigate

1. What do you see in this photo?

   _____

   _____

2. What did you see first? Why?

   _____

   _____

 Question

3. Look at the photo. What do you want to learn more about?

   _____

   _____

4. What is a pueblo?

   _____

   _____

 Understand

5. What is the weather like in the photo?

   _____

   _____

6. How is the girls' home different from your home?

   _____

   _____

Answer Key

Page 7

1. horses, wagon with steam engine, wheels, buildings, hose, people; 2. Answers will vary. 3. Answers will vary. 4. Answers will vary. 5. Three horses are needed to pull the big fire engine. 6. Steam powered the engine that pumped water.

Page 11

1. milk truck, milkman, driver, street, houses, snow; 2. Answers will vary. 3. Answers will vary. 4. Answers will vary. 5. Answers will vary but may include the glass bottles could be reused. 6. Answers will vary.

Page 15

1. plane, man, water; 2. Answers will vary. 3. Answers will vary. 4. Answers will vary. 5. When they were young, they liked things that flew. 6. Answers will vary but may include the pilot is not in a cabin, there is no room for passengers, there are two sets of wings, and there are no wheels.

Page 19

1. Helen Keller, roses, vase, book; 2. Answers will vary. 3. Answers will vary. 4. Answers will vary. 5. Answers will vary but may include it is large with many pages and has no pictures. 6. Answers will vary.

Page 23

1. Answers will vary but may include Ben Franklin, globe, and books. 2-3. Answers will vary. 4. inventor, writer, important American; 5. He showed many things Ben Franklin worked on. 6. Answers will vary.

Page 27

1. George Washington Carver, clump of dirt, land; 2. Answers will vary. 3. Answers will vary. 4. peanut; Answers will vary. 5. He loved plants and growing things. 6. Answers will vary.

Page 31

1. girls in a circle playing, teacher, playground, ball; 2. Answers will vary. 3. Answers will vary. 4. softball, basketball, dodgeball, tennis; 5. dresses, some have no shoes, some have braids and ribbons in their hair; 6. Answers will vary.

Page 35

1. blocks of snow, Inuit family, dogs; 2. Answers will vary. 3. Answers will vary. 4. shelter made of snow; 5. because they traveled and an igloo can be built quickly wherever there is enough snow; 6. because it's cold in Alaska

Page 39

1. teacher, students, dog, desks, chalkboard; 2. Answers will vary. 3. Answers will vary. 4. dog; Answers will vary. 5. They are learning about pets, dogs, animals, or living things. 6. Answers will vary.

Page 43

1. Chief American Horse, feathers, headdress; 2. Answers will vary. 3. Answers will vary. 4. Answers will vary. 5. He is wearing a headdress made of eagle feathers and other special items. 6. shoes made of soft leather; Answers will vary.

Page 47

1. tepees, Chief Charlot's family, mountains; 2. Answers will vary. 3. Answers will vary. 4. a shelter or home; 5. Answers will vary. 6. The woman and girl are wearing dresses and beads. The girl is holding a bag. The chief is holding a shield decorated with feathers.

Page 51

1. baby, girl, cradleboard; 2. Answers will vary. 3. Answers will vary. 4. It is made with wood, leather straps, playthings, and a blanket. 5. pierced its ears, have a party, bless it, give it a cradleboard; 6. tied in with straps and wrapped in blankets

Page 55

1. Jewish boy, store, book, shawl; 2. Answers will vary. 3. Answers will vary. 4. city sidewalk, outside a storefront; 5. to celebrate Rosh Hashanah; 6. pray, go to temple, hear a shofar; eat bread, apples, and honey

Page 59

1. children, rocks, stone building; 2. Answers will vary. 3. Answers will vary. 4. a dragon's head, to celebrate the lunar New Year; 5. They play together. 6. Dragons are a symbol of good luck.

Page 63

1. two girls, pueblo buildings, rug or blanket; 2. Answers will vary. 3. Answers will vary. 4. a shelter or home; 5. hot, dry; 6. Answers will vary.